True Stories
1B

Sandra Heyer

True Stories: Level 1B, Silver Edition

Pearson Education, 221 River Street, Hoboken, NJ 07030

Staff Credits: The people who made up the *True Stories: Level 1B, Silver Edition* team, representing content creation, design, manufacturing, marketing, multimedia, project management, publishing, rights management, and testing, are Pietro Alongi, Tracey Cataldo, Dave Dickey, Warren Fischbach, Lucy Hart, Gosia Jaros-White, Barry Katzen, Linda Moser, Dana Pinter, Paula Van Ells, Joseph Vella, and Peter West.

Text design and layout: Don Williams
Composition: Page Designs International
Project supervision: Bernard Seal
Contributing editor: Bernard Seal

Cover images: *(from top to bottom)* JGI/Tom Grill/Blend Image/Getty Images; Hideki Yoshihara/Aflo Co., Ltd./Alamy Stock Photo; Jevgenia Issakova/123RF; Vacclav/Shutterstock; Tanya Stolyarevskaya/Shutterstock; *(silver edition badge)* deepstock/Shutterstock.
Illustrations: Don Martinetti, Andrés Morales, and Aptara

Library of Congress Cataloging-in-Publication Data

A catalog record for the print edition is available from the Library of Congress.

Printed in the United States of America

ISBN-10: 0-13-517791X
ISBN-13: 978-0-13-517791-4

1   19

CONTENTS

INTRODUCTION

TRUE STORIES, SILVER EDITION

The Silver Edition of *True Stories* is a five-level reading series. The series is appropriate for beginning to high-intermediate learners of English as a Second or Foreign Language. The Silver Edition consists of revised editions of six of the highly successful and popular *True Stories in the News* books that have provided entertaining stories and effective reading skill instruction for many years. In fact, the first book in that series was published over twenty-five years ago (hence the title "Silver" Edition). The *True Stories* series has been going strong ever since.

NEW IN THE SILVER EDITION

- **New and updated stories.** Some stories have been updated, and some have been replaced with fresh new readings that have been thoroughly classroom-tested before making it into print. All of the readings that have proven to be favorites of students and teachers over the years have been retained.

- **A colorful new design.** Originally published solely in black and white, the new edition has a new full-color design with colorful new photos. The color design makes the readings even more inviting, and the color photos that accompany the readings enhance understanding and enjoyment of the stories.

- **A uniform unit structure.** The books in the series have been given a consistent unit structure that runs across all six books. This predictable structure makes it easy for teachers to teach the series at different levels and for students to progress seamlessly from one level to the next.

- **Audio recordings of every reading.** Every story in the series has been recorded and made available online for students or teachers to download.

- **Online Answer Keys and To the Teacher notes.** In addition to being in the back of the books, as they were in the previous editions, the Answer Keys are now also online as downloadable pdfs. The To the Teacher notes that were previously in the back of the books, however, are now only online. This section provides additional information about the stories and teaching tips. Additional practice activities are also now available online.

THE APPROACH

The underlying premise in this series has always been that when second language learners are engaged in a pleasurable reading experience in the second language, then language learning will take place effortlessly and effectively. The formula is simple: Offer students a true story that fascinates and surprises them. Have them read and enjoy the story. Focus their attention on some useful vocabulary in the story. Confirm that they fully understand the story with reading comprehension exercises. Develop reading skills that progress from basic to more complex. Finally, use the content and the topic of the story to engage in discussion and writing tasks, from tightly structured to more open-ended.

UNIT COMPONENTS

Pre-Reading

Each unit begins with a pre-reading task that piques students' curiosity about the content of the story. Students' attention is drawn to the art that accompanies the reading and the title of the reading as they predict what the story is going to be about.

Reading

The readings are short enough to be read by the students in class; at the lower levels, the stories can be read in minutes. As the levels become higher, the readings do become longer and more challenging. Still, even at the highest levels, each reading and the exercises immediately following it can be completed in one class meeting.

Post-Reading

While there is some variation in the post-reading activities, the following are in all six books:

- **Vocabulary.** Useful key vocabulary items are selected from the readings for presentation and practice. The vocabulary activities vary from unit to unit, and the number of vocabulary items and the extent of the practice increases from level to level.

- **Comprehension.** At least two different comprehension tasks follow the vocabulary section. The exercises have descriptive titles, such as Understanding the Main Ideas, Remembering Details, or Understanding Cause and Effect, so that teachers and students know which cognitive skills are being applied. The exercises have a great deal of variety, keeping students engaged and motivated.

- **Discussion.** Having read and studied the stories, students are encouraged to discuss some aspect arising from the story. Even at the lowest level, students are given simple tasks that will give them the opportunity to talk in pairs, in small groups, or as a whole class.

- **Writing.** The final section of each unit has students produce a short piece of writing related to the reading. Often the writing task derives directly from the Discussion, in which case the title of the section is Discussion/Writing. The writing tasks are level-appropriate and vary in complexity depending on student proficiency. The tasks are not intended to be graded. They simply provide a final opportunity for students to engage with the topic of the reading and deepen their understanding and enjoyment of the story.

TRUE STORIES, LEVEL 1B

True Stories, Level 1B, is the second book in the Silver Edition of the *True Stories* series. It is intended for beginning learners of English. It consists of 20 four-page units, each with the following distinguishing features.

- The pre-reading task has students listen to each story while looking at illustrations that recreate the story's narrative.

- Each story has an average length of 275 words.

- There is an overlap in level with *True Stories* 1A to ensure a smooth transition from that book to this.

- The stories are told in the simple present, present progressive, and future tenses, with occasional use of the past tense.

- Writing exercises are sentence completions and composition of single sentences.

ACKNOWLEDGMENTS

I would like to thank

- the many teachers whose invaluable feedback helped me assess how the stories and exercises were working outside the small sphere of my own classroom. If I were to list you all by name, this acknowledgments section would go on for pages. I would like to thank three colleagues in particular: legendary teacher Peggy Miles, who introduced me to the world of English language teaching; Sharron Bassano, whose innovative techniques for teaching beginning-level students informed my own approach; and Jorge Islas Martinez, whose enthusiasm and dedication remain a constant inspiration;

- my students, who shared personal stories that became the examples for the discussion and writing exercises;

- the people in the stories who supplied details that were not in news sources: Twyla Thompson, John Koehler, Dorothy Peckham, Chi Hsii Tsui, Margaret Patrick, Trish Moore and Rhonda Gill (grandmother and mother of Desiree), Friendship Force participants, Natalie Garibian, Mirsada Buric, and the late Irvin Scott;

- the teachers and editors who made important contributions at different stages of development to the previous editions of these books and whose influence can still be seen throughout this new edition: Allen Ascher, John Barnes, Karen Davy, Joanne Dresner, Nancy Hayward, Stacey Hunter, Penny LaPorte, Laura LeDrean, Françoise Leffler, Linda Moser, Dana Klinek Pinter, Mary Perrotta Rich, Debbie Sistino, and Paula Van Ells;

- Rachel Hayward and Megan Hohenstein, who assisted in piloting and researching new material for the Silver Edition;

- the team at Pearson, whose experienced hands skillfully put together all the moving pieces in the preparation of this Silver Edition: Pietro Alongi, Tracey Cataldo, Warren Fischbach, Lucy Hart, Gosia Jaros-White, Linda Moser, Dana Pinter, Joseph Vella, and Peter West;

- copyeditor and fact checker, Kate Smyres; and proofreader, Ann Dickson;

- editor extraordinaire Françoise Leffler, who lent her expertise to *True Stories* levels 4 and 5;

- Bernard Seal at Page Designs International, who guided this project from start to finish with dedication, creativity, pragmatism, and the occasional "crazy"—but brilliant—idea;

- Don Williams at Page Designs International, whose talent for design is evident on every page; and

- my husband, John Hajdu Heyer, who read the first draft of every story I've considered for the *True Stories* series. The expression on his face as he read told me whether or not the story was a keeper. He didn't know that. Now he does.

FROM THE AUTHOR

Dear Teachers and Students,

This new edition of *True Stories* is the Silver Edition because it celebrates an anniversary— it has been more than 25 years since the first *True Stories* book was published. The way we get our news has changed a lot over the years, but some things have remained the same: Fascinating stories are in the news every day, and the goal of the *True Stories* series is still to bring the best of them to you.

The question students ask most often about these stories is *Are they true?* The answer is *yes*—to the best of my knowledge, these stories are true. I've fact-checked stories by contacting reporters, photojournalists, and research librarians all over the world. I've even called some of the people in the stories to be sure I have the facts right.

Once I'm as sure as I can be that a story is true, the story has to pass one more test. My students read the story, and after they finish reading, they give each story one, two, or three stars. They take this responsibility seriously; they know that only the top-rated stories will become part of the *True Stories* reading series.

I hope that you, too, think these are three-star stories. And I hope that reading them encourages you to share your own stories, which are always the most amazing true stories of all.

Sandra Heyer

UNIT 1

1 PRE-READING

Look at the pictures. Listen to your teacher tell the story.

Hawaiian Vacation

Quentin Gwynn

Quentin Gwynn is in Hawaii with friends. He is on vacation, and he is having a wonderful time.

One afternoon Quentin is standing on a high rock. He is looking at the ocean. He sees a boy in the water below. The boy is in trouble. He is far from the beach, and he can't swim. Quentin takes off his backpack and his shoes. Then he jumps into the water, swims to the boy, and pulls him to the beach.

The boy isn't breathing. Quentin gives him CPR, and the boy begins to breathe again. Later, an ambulance comes. Paramedics check the boy. "He is fine," the paramedics tell Quentin. "You saved his life."

Quentin walks back to the high rock. His shoes are there, but his backpack is gone. Quentin's credit cards, his camera, and his money were in the backpack. "Well," Quentin thinks, "this is the end of my vacation."

Quentin's story is in the newspaper. People read about Quentin and the boy. They also read about Quentin's backpack.

A hotel owner tells Quentin, "Your room here is free." Restaurant owners tell Quentin, "Your meals here are free." A lot of people give Quentin money. "Here's money for a new camera," the people say. "Buy some other things, too. Have fun in Hawaii."

So it is not the end of Quentin's vacation. He stays in Hawaii an extra week. He has a wonderful time.

2 VOCABULARY

Write the correct word on the line.

credit card	CPR	free	gone	in trouble	meals

1. The boy in the water is far from the beach, and he can't swim. That is dangerous. Quentin sees that the boy is ___*in trouble*___.

2. Quentin pushes on the boy's chest five times. Then he breathes into the boy's mouth. He does this many times. Quentin is giving the boy _____.

3. When Quentin goes back to the high rock, his backpack is not there. It is _____.

4. When Quentin buys something, he doesn't always pay with cash. Sometimes he pays with a _____.

5. Quentin doesn't pay for his hotel room. It is _____.

6. Quentin doesn't pay for his breakfast, lunch, or dinner. All his _____ are free, too.

3 COMPREHENSION

UNDERSTANDING THE MAIN IDEAS

Answer the questions. Circle *a* or *b*.

1. Where is Quentin?
   a. He is on vacation in Hawaii.
   b. He is on vacation in Mexico.

2. Who gives the boy CPR?
   a. Paramedics give the boy CPR.
   b. Quentin gives the boy CPR.

3. What happens to Quentin's backpack?
   a. Someone takes it.
   b. He leaves it at the hotel.

4. What is in Quentin's backpack?
   a. His credit cards, his camera, and his money are in his backpack.
   b. His sunglasses, his camera, and a map of Hawaii are in his backpack.

5. What do people give Quentin?
   a. They give him a free plane ticket home.
   b. They give him a free hotel room, free meals, and money.

UNDERSTANDING SEQUENCE

Which happens first? Write _1_ on the line. Which happens second? Write _2_ on the line.

1. __2__ Quentin pulls the boy to the beach.

   __1__ Quentin jumps into the water.

2. _____ Quentin gives the boy CPR.

   _____ The boy begins to breathe again.

3. _____ Paramedics tell Quentin the boy is fine.

   _____ An ambulance comes.

4. _____ Someone takes Quentin's backpack.

   _____ Quentin's story is in the newspaper.

5. _____ People give Quentin money.

   _____ Quentin stays in Hawaii an extra week.

4 DISCUSSION / WRITING

A With your classmates, talk about good places to have a vacation: Hawaii? Acapulco? Paris? Make a list on the board.

B Choose one of the places on the board. On your own paper, write four sentences about it. (Do not write the name of the place on your paper.) For example:

1. It is hot there.
2. There are beautiful beaches.
3. Many people go there to see the sunset.
4. Young men dive into the ocean from high rocks.

C Tape your paper to a wall in your classroom.

D Walk around the room. Read the sentences on each paper. Which place do the sentences describe? If you think you know, write the place on the paper.

E Take your paper off the wall and read your sentences to the class. Tell the class the name of the place you described.

UNIT 2

1 PRE-READING

Look at the pictures. Listen to your teacher tell the story.

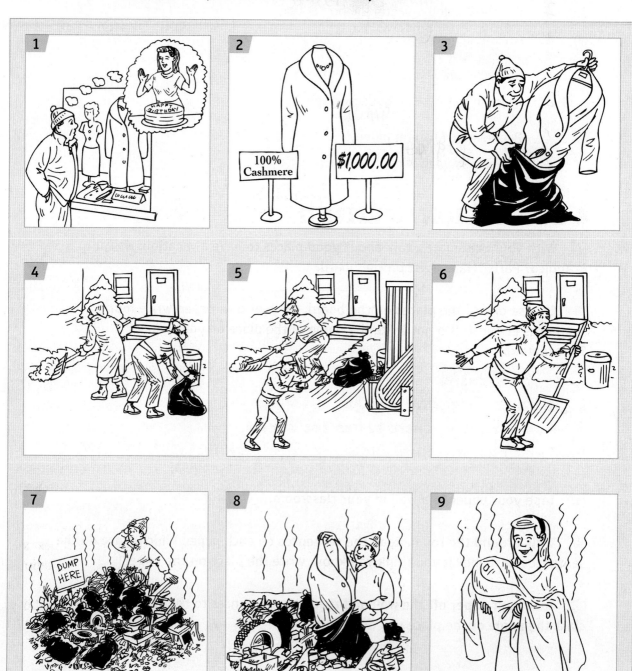

The Birthday Present

Joe is shopping. He is looking for a present for his wife. Her birthday is in two days.

He sees a coat. It is a warm coat, and it is beautiful. It is also expensive—$1,000. Joe is not a rich man. But he loves the coat, and he loves his wife, so he buys the coat.

Joe doesn't want his wife to see the coat, so he puts it in a black plastic bag. Then he takes the coat to his brother's house.

When Joe arrives at his brother's house, his sister-in-law is outside shoveling snow. "I'll help you," Joe says. He puts the black plastic bag down on the snow.

While Joe is shoveling snow, a garbage truck comes. The men see the black plastic bag on the snow. They pick it up and throw it into the truck.

When Joe finishes shoveling the snow, he looks for the black plastic bag. It is gone! Then Joe remembers the garbage truck. "Oh, no!" he thinks. "Maybe the black plastic bag is in the garbage truck!"

The garbage truck takes garbage to the dump. So Joe drives to the dump. There are thousands of black plastic bags at the dump. Which one has the coat in it? For hours, Joe opens black plastic bags. He finds empty boxes and cans. He finds old shoes and clothes. He finds old potatoes and onions. Finally, he finds the coat.

Joe gives the coat to his wife on her birthday. "It's beautiful!" she says. "I love it! But…"

"But what?" Joe asks.

"It smells like onions."

2 VOCABULARY

Write the correct word on the line.

dump	empty	gone	present	shoveling	sister-in-law

1. Joe wants to give his wife something. He is looking for a
   _____*present*_____ for her.

2. Joe's brother is married. When Joe arrives at his brother's house, his brother's
   wife is outside working. Joe helps his _____.

3. It is a cold winter day, and Joe's sister-in-law is _____ snow.

4. Joe looks everywhere for the black plastic bag, but he can't find it. The bag
   is _____.

5. The garbage trucks take all the garbage to the _____.

6. Joe finds boxes and cans with nothing in them. They are _____.

3 COMPREHENSION

UNDERSTANDING THE MAIN IDEAS

Complete the sentences. Circle *a* or *b*.

1. Joe is looking for a present for his wife because
   a. she is in the hospital.
   b. her birthday is in two days.

2. Joe buys the expensive coat because
   a. he loves his wife.
   b. he is a rich man.

3. Joe puts the coat in a black plastic bag because
   a. he doesn't want the coat to get dirty.
   b. he doesn't want his wife to see it.

4. Joe doesn't see the garbage truck because
   a. he is watching TV.
   b. he is shoveling snow.

5. The coat smells like onions because
   a. it was at the garbage dump.
   b. Joe's wife is cooking onions.

REMEMBERING DETAILS

What does Joe find at the dump? Circle seven words.

(empty boxes)	old shoes	an old chair
old onions	empty cans	old clothes
an old bicycle	old potatoes	the coat

4 DISCUSSION

Joe buys a birthday present for his wife. It is a warm, beautiful, and expensive coat.

With your classmates, make a list of presents people like to give and receive. Your teacher will write your list on the board.

5 WRITING

A Write your name on a piece of paper. Fold it and put it in a box. Your classmates will put their names in the box, too. Reach into the box and take a piece of paper.

B Choose a present for the student whose name is on your piece of paper. Complete the letter below. Then deliver it to your classmate.

Dear _____,

    I want to give you _____ for a present

because _____.

                      Your friend,

                      _____

C You have a letter from a classmate with a "present." Complete this thank-you note on your own paper. Then deliver it to the person who gave you the present.

Dear _____,

    Thank you very much for _____. I liked the

present because _____.

                      Your friend,

                      _____

UNIT 3

1 PRE-READING

Look at the pictures. Listen to your teacher tell the story.

Anna's Choice

Anna is talking to her father. "Papa," Anna says. "I'm in love, and I want to get married. I want to marry Iztok."

"Iztok!" Anna's father says. "No! You can't marry Iztok. He's an artist. Artists don't make a lot of money. You're only 18 years old. I know what's best for you. Marry an engineer. Engineers make a lot of money."

Anna tells Iztok, "I can't marry you. I'm going to marry an engineer."

Iztok is silent for a few minutes. Then he kisses Anna. "OK," he tells Anna. "Marry your engineer. Maybe he can make money. But can he kiss?" Iztok walks away.

Anna marries an engineer. She and her husband have three children. But Anna is not happy. She thinks about Iztok every day.

Iztok gets married, too. He and his wife have two children. But Iztok is not happy. He thinks about Anna every day.

Twenty-six years go by. Anna's children grow up and move away. She and her husband get divorced. Her father dies. Anna is alone now. She wonders about Iztok. Is he still married? Or is he alone now, too? She hires a private detective. "Look for Iztok," Anna tells the detective.

The detective finds Iztok. He is living in another city, and he is divorced. "Anna is looking for you," the detective tells Iztok.

Ten days later, Iztok visits Anna, and they decide to get married. Anna is 44 years old, and Iztok is 51. They are not young. But they are still in love. And they are finally happy.

2 VOCABULARY

Write the opposites. You can find the words in the story.

1. mother   _f_ _a_ _t_ _h_ _e_ _r_

2. can   _c_ _a_ _n_ _'_ _t_

3. a little   __ __ __ __

4. old   __ __ __ __ __

5. wife   __ __ __ __ __ __ __

6. divorce   __ __ __ __ __ __

3 COMPREHENSION

REMEMBERING DETAILS

Which sentence is correct? Circle *a* or *b*.

1. (a.) Anna's father says, "You can't marry Iztok!"
   b. Anna's mother says, "You can't marry Iztok!"

2. a. Iztok is a mechanic.
   b. Iztok is an artist.

3. a. Anna is 24 years old.
   b. Anna is 18 years old.

4. a. Anna marries an engineer.
   b. Anna marries a doctor.

5. a. Anna is happy.
   b. Anna is not happy.

6. a. Iztok thinks about Anna every day.
   b. Iztok never thinks about Anna.

7. a. The years go by, and Anna forgets Iztok.
   b. The years go by, and Anna wonders about Iztok.

8. a. Iztok is living in another country.
   b. Iztok is living in another city.

WHO SAYS IT?

Who says it? Write the letter of your answer on the line. You will use some answers two times.

_c_ 1. "I'm in love, and I want to get married."

_____ 2. "Artists don't make a lot of money."

_____ 3. "I know what's best for you."

_____ 4. "I can't marry you."

_____ 5. "Marry your engineer. Maybe he can make money."

_____ 6. "Anna is looking for you."

a. Anna's father

b. the private detective

c. Anna

d. Iztok

4 DISCUSSION / WRITING

Anna's father says, "You can't marry Iztok. He's an artist. Artists don't make a lot of money."

A Why do parents sometimes tell their children, "Don't marry him" or "Don't marry her"? On the lines below, write as many reasons as you can. For example:

He or she is too old.
He or she doesn't have a job.

_____

_____

_____

_____

_____

_____

B In a small group, share your sentences. Discuss if you think the reasons are good or bad.

UNIT 4

1 PRE-READING

Look at the pictures. Listen to your teacher tell the story.

Hold On, Joe

The rescue of Joe Thompson

Joe Thompson is 18 years old, and he drives a small Jeep. Joe loves to drive his car. Sometimes he wears his seat belt. Sometimes he doesn't.

One day Joe is driving his Jeep. He is not wearing his seat belt. Suddenly another car turns in front of him. Joe hits the other car. Joe's Jeep rolls over once, twice, three times, four times. The fourth time the Jeep rolls over, the top comes off. Joe goes up into the air. He goes up high.

There are some wires above the street. One wire catches Joe's foot. He grabs another wire with his hand. Now Joe is hanging high above the street. He is holding onto the wires. Joe is lucky: These wires are not for electricity; they are for telephones.

Joe has a cell phone in his pocket. He calls 911. Then he calls his father. "I had an accident," he tells his father. "I'm hanging from some wires high above the street."

"Hold on, Joe," his father says. "Hold on."

Twenty minutes later, rescue workers take Joe down from the wires. Then they take him to the hospital. A doctor at the hospital tells Joe, "You are fine—no cuts, no broken bones. You can go home."

A few weeks later, Joe buys a new Jeep. He loves to drive his car. He always wears his seat belt.

2 VOCABULARY

Match the words and the pictures. Write your answer on the line.

hit	hold on	roll over	seat belt	turn	wires

1. _____turn_____   2. _____   3. _____

4. _____   5. _____   6. _____

3 COMPREHENSION

MAKING CONNECTIONS

Complete the sentences. Write the letter of your answer on the line.

1. Another car turns __c__

2. Joe goes up ____

3. Joe grabs a wire ____

4. Joe has a cell phone ____

5. Joe is hanging ____

6. Rescue workers take Joe ____

a. in his pocket.

b. to the hospital.

c. in front of Joe.

d. from some wires above the street.

e. into the air.

f. with his hand

UNDERSTANDING SEQUENCE

Which happens first? Write *1* on the line. Which happens second? Write *2* on the line.

1. __2__ Joe hits the car.

   __1__ A car turns in front of Joe.

2. ____ The Jeep rolls over once, twice, three times, four times.

   ____ The top comes off the Jeep.

3. ____ Joe grabs a wire with his hand.

   ____ Joe goes up into the air.

4. ____ Joe calls his father.

   ____ Joe calls 911.

4 DISCUSSION / WRITING

A **Walk around the room. Ask five people the question below. Write each person's name on the line. Check (✓) their answers.**

Do you wear a seat belt?

Name	Always	Usually	Never
1. _____	☐	☐	☐
2. _____	☐	☐	☐
3. _____	☐	☐	☐
4. _____	☐	☐	☐
5. _____	☐	☐	☐

B **On your own paper, write sentences with the information above. For example:**

Jingjing always wears a seat belt.
Aldo usually wears a seat belt.
Mary never wears a seat belt.

UNIT 5

1 PRE-READING

Look at the pictures. Listen to your teacher tell the story.

A Problem with Monkeys

An old woman is walking home. She is carrying a bag of groceries. Suddenly a monkey takes the groceries and runs.

Where does this happen? This happens in Hong Kong. Hong Kong is a big city with a big problem—a problem with monkeys.

More than 2,000 monkeys live in a forest near Hong Kong. Signs in the forest say, "DO NOT FEED THE MONKEYS." But people like to go to the forest and feed the monkeys. They give the monkeys peanuts, potato chips, chocolate, and bread. The monkeys like that food! So, they go into the city to get it.

The monkeys take bags of groceries from old women. They take bread from babies. They go into apartments through open windows and take fruit from kitchen tables.

In some apartments, the monkeys find cans of beer. They open the cans and drink the beer.

Most people in Hong Kong don't want the monkeys in their city. They say, "Hong Kong is not a good place for monkeys. The forest is a good place for monkeys."

But the monkeys don't want to eat in the forest. There is no bread in the forest. And there is no beer!

Every day the monkeys come into the city. How can the city of Hong Kong stop them? People know that they must not feed the monkeys, but they still do it. So Hong Kong is a big city with *two* big problems: a problem with monkeys, and a problem with people!

2 VOCABULARY

Match the words and the pictures. Write your answer on the line.

| carry | feed | forest | groceries | sign | through |

1. _____carry_____ 2. _____ 3. _____

4. _____ 5. _____ 6. _____

3 COMPREHENSION

REMEMBERING DETAILS

What do the monkeys do in Hong Kong? Check (✓) five answers. The first one is done for you.

- ☑ 1. They take bags of groceries from old women.
- ☐ 2. They take bread from babies.
- ☐ 3. They watch TV.
- ☐ 4. They go into apartments through open windows.
- ☐ 5. They try on clothes.
- ☐ 6. They take fruit from kitchen tables.
- ☐ 7. They take money out of pockets.
- ☐ 8. They open cans of beer.

REVIEWING THE STORY

Write the correct word on the line.

This story ____*happens*____ in Hong Kong. Hong Kong is a big city with
          1.

a big _____. More than 2,000 monkeys live in a forest
          2.

_____ Hong Kong. People go to the forest and give peanuts,
      3.

potato chips, chocolate, and bread to the monkeys. People know that they

_____ not feed the monkeys, but they still do it. The monkeys like
      4.

the "people food," so they go into the _____ to get it.
                            5.

4 DISCUSSION / WRITING

A   Are these animals a problem in your native city? Circle the pictures of the problem animals. (Is there another problem animal in your city? Draw a picture of it in the box and write its name on the line.) Why are these animals a problem? Tell the class.

rats   cockroaches   dogs   birds

_____
(Write the name of another
problem animal here.)

B   Make sentences with the information above. For example:

We don't have a problem with rats.
We have a problem with cockroaches.

1. _____

2. _____

3. _____

4. _____

5. _____

UNIT 6

1 PRE-READING

Look at the pictures. Listen to your teacher tell the story.

Alone for 43 Years

It is 1947. In a small town in Russia, some people are talking. They are talking about their leader. His name is Joseph Stalin.

"Stalin is not a good leader," a young man says. The young man's name is Ivan.

Suddenly everyone is silent. It is dangerous to say, "Stalin is not a good leader." The people look around. They see a policeman. The policeman is listening to them.

Ivan is afraid. "Maybe I will go to prison," he thinks. He runs home. He throws some clothes, some tools, and some pans into a bag. Then he runs into the forest.

Ivan runs for 18 hours. Then he sleeps. When he wakes up, he gets out his tools—a hammer, a saw, and some nails—and he builds a small house.

Ivan lives in the small house in the forest. He drinks water from a river. He eats rabbits and berries. He is very lonely, but he doesn't go home. He is afraid.

Ivan lives in the forest for 43 years. Then, in 1990, his family visits him. "Come home, Ivan," they say. "Russia is different. Stalin is dead, and Russia has new leaders."

Ivan doesn't believe them, so they give him a newspaper.

Ivan reads the newspaper. "Yes," he says. "Russia is different now."

And finally, after 43 years alone, Ivan goes home.

2 VOCABULARY

Which words go together? Connect them with a line.

1.	1947		country
2.	Russia		year
3.	Joseph Stalin		family
4.	pants, shirt, dress		leader
5.	rabbit		tools
6.	berries		animal
7.	sister, father, cousin		clothes
8.	hammer, saw, nails		fruit

3 COMPREHENSION

REMEMBERING DETAILS

One word in each sentence is not correct. Find the word and cross it out. Then choose the correct word and write it above the mistake.

afraid	dangerous	leader	man	pans	Russia	small	years

1. In a small town in ~~China~~, *Russia* some people are talking.

2. They are talking about Joseph Stalin, their friend.

3. "Stalin is not a good leader," a young woman says.

4. It is OK to say, "Stalin is not a good leader."

5. Ivan is happy; he thinks, "Maybe I will go to prison."

6. He throws some clothes, some tools, and some photos into a bag.

7. He builds a big house in the forest.

8. He lives in the forest for 43 days.

UNDERSTANDING SEQUENCE

Which happens first? Write *1* on the line. Which happens second? Write *2* on the line.

1. __1__ Ivan says, "Stalin is not a good leader."
   __2__ The people see a policeman.

2. _____ Ivan runs into the forest.
   _____ Ivan throws some clothes, some tools, and some pans into a bag.

3. _____ Ivan builds a house.
   _____ Ivan runs for 18 hours.

4. _____ Ivan goes home.
   _____ Ivan's family gives him a newspaper.

4 DISCUSSION / WRITING

Joseph Stalin was the leader of Russia from 1929 to 1953.

A **Write some sentences about a leader of a country—past or present. For example:**

Queen Isabella was an important Spanish leader.
She lived from 1451 to 1504.
Her husband was King Ferdinand.
Queen Isabella gave money to Christopher Columbus.

1. _____
2. _____
3. _____
4. _____
5. _____

B **Read your sentences aloud to the class. Don't say the name of the leader— say *she* or *he*. Your classmates will try to guess the leader's name.**

UNIT 7

1 PRE-READING

Look at the pictures. Listen to your teacher tell the story.

An Easy Job

Anne wants to put new vinyl on her kitchen floor. It is a small floor, so Anne thinks, "This is an easy job. I can do it myself."

First, Anne spreads glue on the floor. Then she carries in the vinyl. Whoops! She falls down. She falls right into the glue. The glue is on Anne's hands and legs, but Anne doesn't stop to clean it off. "I can clean the glue off later," Anne thinks. She wants to put down the vinyl before the glue on the floor dries. Quickly, Anne puts the vinyl on the floor. It looks great. "That was easy!" Anne thinks.

Now Anne remembers the glue on her hands and legs. How can she take it off? She sits down and calls a friend. "Do you know how to clean off glue?" she asks her friend.

"Sorry," her friend says. "I don't know."

"Well, thanks anyway," Anne says. "Bye."

When she finishes talking, Anne tries to put down her phone. She can't. Her right hand is glued to the phone. Then she tries to stand up. She can't. Her legs are glued to the chair. Anne needs help. She tries to call 911 with her left hand. She can't. Her left hand is glued to her left leg. She uses her nose to call 911.

Firefighters arrive. Firefighters usually fight fires—they don't usually fight glue. But they know what to do. They have a special cleaner. It takes off glue. Three firefighters clean the glue off Anne. It takes them one hour. It is not an easy job!

2 VOCABULARY

Write the correct word or words on the line.

anyway	myself	put down	quickly	spreads	take off

1. Anne thinks, "This is an easy job. I don't need help. I can do

   it _____*myself*_____."

2. Anne puts the glue everywhere on the floor. She _____

   the glue.

3. Anne works fast. She puts the vinyl on the floor _____.

4. Anne doesn't want glue on her hands and legs. She wants to

   _____ the glue.

5. Anne's friend has no information about cleaning off glue. So Anne doesn't say,

   "Thank you for your help." She says, "Thanks _____."

6. When Anne finishes her conversation, she wants to _____

   the phone.

3 COMPREHENSION

UNDERSTANDING THE MAIN IDEAS

Answer the questions. Circle *a* or *b*.

1. What job does Anne want to do?
   - (a.) She wants to put new vinyl on her kitchen floor.
   - b. She wants to paint her kitchen.

2. Why does Anne think, "This is an easy job"?
   - a. It is a small floor.
   - b. Anne works with vinyl every day.

3. Who comes to clean the glue off Anne?
   - a. Firefighters come.
   - b. Anne's friends come.

4. How long does it take to clean off the glue?
   - a. It takes three hours.
   - b. It takes one hour.

FINDING MORE INFORMATION

Read each sentence on the left. Which sentence on the right gives you more information? Write the letter of your answer on the line.

_d_ 1. Anne wants to put new vinyl on her kitchen floor.

_____ 2. Anne falls down.

_____ 3. Anne calls a friend.

_____ 4. The firefighters have a special cleaner.

_____ 5. The firefighters clean the glue off Anne.

a. It takes off glue.

b. It takes them one hour.

c. "Do you know how to clean off glue?" she asks.

d It is a small floor.

e. She falls right into the glue.

4 DISCUSSION / WRITING

A What jobs can you do in your house? With your classmates, make a list. Your teacher will write your list on the board. For example:

Kai   put vinyl on the floor
Yumiko   paint

B Work with a partner. Use the information on the board to ask your partner questions. For example:

Can you paint? Yes, I can. **OR** *No, I can't. But Yumiko can.*

C On the lines below, write five sentences with the information on the board. For example:

Kai can put vinyl on the floor.
Yumiko can paint.

1. _____

2. _____

3. _____

4. _____

5. _____

UNIT 8

1 PRE-READING

Look at the pictures. Listen to your teacher tell the story.

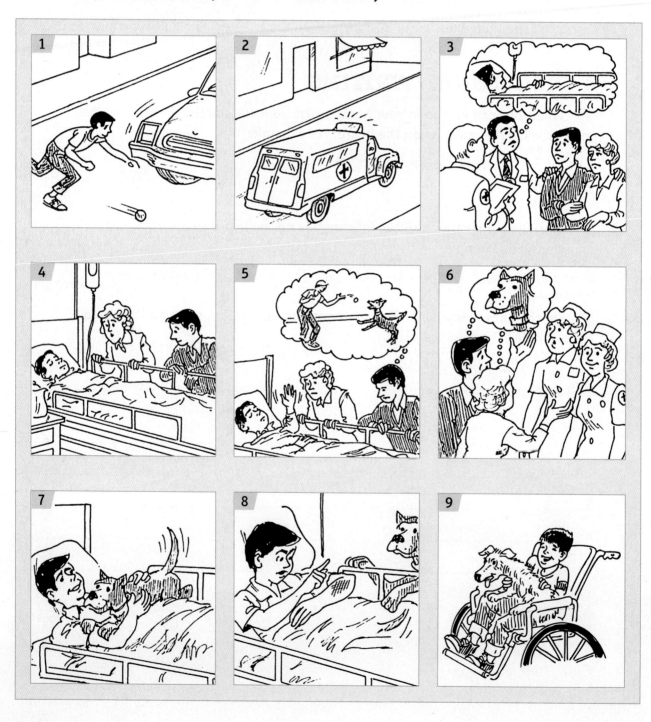

The Power of Love

Donny, an 11-year-old boy, is playing with a ball. The ball goes into the street, and Donny runs for the ball. A car hits Donny.

An ambulance takes Donny to the hospital. The doctors at the hospital tell Donny's parents, "Donny is in a coma. Maybe he will wake up tomorrow. Maybe he will wake up next week. Or maybe he will never wake up."

Every day Donny's parents visit him at the hospital. They sit next to Donny's bed and talk to him. But Donny never talks to them. He just sleeps.

One day Donny's father says, "Wake up, Donny. Wake up and come home. Come home and play with Rusty." Rusty is Donny's dog.

When Donny's father says "Rusty," Donny moves his arm.

"Rusty!" Donny's father says again. Again, Donny moves his arm.

Donny's parents have an idea. They tell the nurses, "We want to bring Donny's dog to the hospital. Is it OK?"

"A dog in the hospital?" the nurses say. "That's very unusual. But, yes, it's OK."

The next day, Donny's parents bring Rusty to the hospital. When they put the dog on Donny's bed, Donny opens his eyes and hugs the dog.

Donny's parents bring Rusty to the hospital every day. One day, Rusty jumps on Donny's bed and scratches Donny's arm. Donny says his first words: "Bad dog!"

After seven weeks, Donny is well. He leaves the hospital and goes home. Rusty goes home with him.

2 VOCABULARY

Match the pictures and the sentences. Write the letter of your answer on the line.

a. Donny *hugs* the dog.

b. A car *hits* Donny.

c. Donny is in a *coma*.

d. Rusty *scratches* Donny's arm.

e. An *ambulance* takes Donny to the hospital.

f. Donny *moves* his arm.

1. __b__

2. ____

3. ____

4. ____

5. ____

6. ____

3 COMPREHENSION

UNDERSTANDING SEQUENCE

Which happens first? Write *1* on the line. Which happens second? Write *2* on the line.

1. __2__ A car hits Donny.

   __1__ Donny runs for the ball.

2. ____ Donny's parents visit him at the hospital.

   ____ An ambulance takes Donny to the hospital.

3. ____ Donny's father says, "Come home and play with Rusty."

   ____ Donny moves his arm.

4. ____ Donny's parents bring Rusty to the hospital.

   ____ Donny's parents tell the nurses, "We want to bring Donny's dog to the hospital."

WHO SAYS IT?

Who says it? Write the letter of your answer on the line.

_b_   1. "Donny is in a coma."

____   2. "Come home and play with Rusty."

____   3. "We want to bring Donny's dog to the hospital. Is it OK?"

____   4. "That's very unusual. But, yes, it's OK."

____   5. "Bad dog!"

a. Donny

b. the doctors

c. Donny's parents

d. Donny's father

e. the nurses

4 DISCUSSION / WRITING

Donny's father says "Rusty," and Donny begins to wake up from the coma.

A Imagine this: You are in a coma. What can help you wake up? The smell of your favorite food? Your favorite music? The voice of a friend or someone in your family? Make a list on the lines below. For example, these things helped people in a coma wake up:

• a song by Adele

• the smell of a spice

• hearing a funny family story

_____

_____

_____

_____

_____

_____

B Share your list in a small group. Explain why the things on your list can help you wake up from a coma.

UNIT 9

1 PRE-READING

Look at the pictures. Listen to your teacher tell the story.

The Pet Rabbit

Mrs. Nunn is at the supermarket with her three children. She looks worried. Her husband has no work, and she has only a little money for food.

A young man is working at the supermarket. His name is Jeff. Jeff is throwing old vegetables into a box. "What are you going to do with those vegetables?" Mrs. Nunn asks.

"I'm going to throw them in the garbage," Jeff says.

"Can I have them?" Mrs. Nunn asks. "We have a pet rabbit. I can give the vegetables to the rabbit."

"Sure, you can have the vegetables," Jeff says. He gives Mrs. Nunn a big box of old vegetables.

The Nunn family doesn't really have a pet rabbit. Mrs. Nunn wants the old vegetables to make soup for her family.

Every week Jeff gives Mrs. Nunn a box of vegetables for the "rabbit." Sometimes Mrs. Nunn finds cans of soup under the vegetables. Sometimes she finds soap, juice, or baby food.

When Mrs. Nunn goes to the supermarket one day, Jeff is not there. He doesn't work at the supermarket anymore. But it doesn't matter. Mrs. Nunn's husband is working again. She doesn't need the old vegetables.

Ten years go by. Mrs. Nunn is shopping at the supermarket when she sees Jeff. He is standing in the store's office. He is the store manager now.

"Mrs. Nunn!" Jeff says. "I think of you and your family often." Then he asks quietly, "How is the rabbit?"

"Thank you for asking," Mrs. Nunn says and smiles. "The rabbit left a long time ago. We are all doing fine."

2 VOCABULARY

Write the correct word on the line.

| anymore | it doesn't matter | manager | pet | quietly | worried |

1. Mrs. Nunn is thinking, "My children are hungry. But I have only a little money. How can I buy food for my children?" She is _____*worried*_____.

2. Mrs. Nunn says, "We have a rabbit. It lives in our house. It is a _____ rabbit."

3. Jeff has a new job now. He works at a different place. He doesn't work at the supermarket _____.

4. One day Mrs. Nunn goes to the supermarket, and Jeff is not there. There are no boxes of vegetables for her, but it is not a problem. Her husband is working now, so _____.

5. Ten years later, Mrs. Nunn goes to the supermarket and sees Jeff. He is a boss at the supermarket. He is the store _____.

6. Jeff doesn't want other people to hear his conversation with Mrs. Nunn. So he asks _____, "How is the rabbit?"

3 COMPREHENSION

UNDERSTANDING THE MAIN IDEAS

Answer the questions. Circle *a* or *b*.

1. Who is Jeff?
   a. He is Mrs. Nunn's husband.
   (b.) He is a young man who works at the supermarket.

2. Why is Jeff throwing old vegetables into a box?
   a. He is going to give them to poor people.
   b. He is going to throw them in the garbage.

3. Why does Mrs. Nunn want the old vegetables?
   a. She wants to sell them.
   b. She wants to make soup.

4. Why does Mrs. Nunn say, "I can give the vegetables to the rabbit"?
   a. She doesn't want Jeff to know the vegetables are for her family.
   b. She has a pet rabbit, and the rabbit is always hungry.

5. Why does Jeff put soup, soap, juice, and baby food under the vegetables?

    a. He knows rabbits like these things.

    b. He knows Mrs. Nunn needs these things for her family.

UNDERSTANDING DIALOGUE

Match the questions and the answers. Write the letter of your answer on the line.

_c_ 1. "What are you going to do with those vegetables?"

_____ 2. "Can I have the old vegetables?"

_____ 3. "How is the rabbit?"

_____ 4. "How are you and your family?"

a. "Sure, you can have them."

b. "Thank you for asking. We are all doing fine."

c. "I'm going to throw them in the garbage."

d. "It left a long time ago."

4 DISCUSSION/WRITING

When people have only a little money, they can't buy expensive food.

A Think about a dinner that is delicious but not expensive. Draw a picture of it in the box on the right.

B Write three sentences about the dinner. For example:

This is a salad. It is potatoes, carrots, corn, and tuna mixed together with mayonnaise. It is good in hot weather.

_____

_____

_____

C Show your picture to a partner. Tell your partner about the delicious dinner.

UNIT 10

1 PRE-READING

Look at the pictures. Listen to your teacher tell the story.

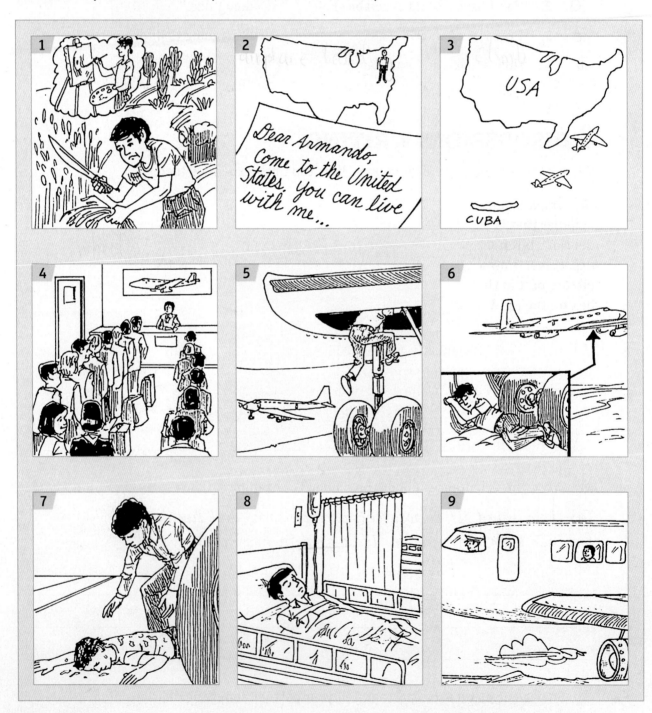

The Escape

Armando and his uncle

Armando lives in Cuba. He works in the fields every day. Armando doesn't want to work in the fields. He wants to be an artist.

Armando wants to go to the United States. His uncle lives in the United States. Armando's uncle writes him letters. "Come," his uncle writes. "You can live with me. You can study art."

But how can Armando go to the United States? It is impossible! Only two planes fly to the United States every day. More than 800,000 people are waiting for tickets.

One day Armando goes to the airport in Havana. He sees a big plane on the runway. It is waiting to take off. Nobody is near the plane. Armando runs to the plane and climbs up by the wheels.

The plane takes off and flies east. Armando and the plane are going to Spain.

The plane flies high over the ocean. The temperature is −40 degrees Celsius. Armando is wearing only pants and a cotton shirt. He is very cold. He is tired, too. He falls asleep.

Nine hours later, the plane lands in Spain. Mechanics are checking the plane when something falls from the wheels. It is Armando! There is ice on Armando's clothes, hands, and face. Armando is unconscious, but he is alive.

Armando stays in a hospital in Spain for two weeks. Then he flies to the United States. This time, he flies *inside* the plane.

2 VOCABULARY

Match the words and the pictures. Write your answer on the line.

| airplane landing | airplane taking off | climb | field | runway | wheel |

1. _____ *runway* _____

2. _____

3. _____

4. _____

5. _____

6. _____

3 COMPREHENSION

MAKING CONNECTIONS

Find the best way to complete each sentence. Write the letter of your answer on the line.

1. Armando lives __*c*__

2. Armando works _____

3. Armando wants to go _____

4. Armando's uncle says, "You can live _____

5. Armando and the plane fly _____

6. Mechanics are checking the plane when something falls _____

7. There is ice _____

8. When Armando flies to the United States, he flies _____

a. to Spain.

b. inside the plane.

c. in Cuba.

d. from the wheels.

e. to the United States.

f. on Armando's clothes, hands, and face.

g. with me."

h. in the fields.

REMEMBERING DETAILS

One word in each sentence is not correct. Find the word and cross it out. Then choose the correct word and write it above the mistake.

east	Havana	ocean	shirt	temperature	wheels

1. One day Armando goes to the airport in ~~Lima~~. *Havana*

2. Armando runs to a plane and climbs up by the windows.

3. The plane takes off and flies north.

4. The plane flies high over the forest.

5. The time is –40 degrees Celsius.

6. Armando is wearing only pants and a cotton jacket.

4 DISCUSSION / WRITING

Armando wants to be an artist. That is his "dream job."

A Answer the questions about your dream job. Write your answers on the lines.

1. What is your dream job? _____

2. What time do you start work in the morning? _____

3. What time do you stop work? _____

4. How long is your lunch break? _____

5. How long is your vacation? _____

B Share your writing in a small group. Compare your idea of a dream job with your classmates' ideas.

UNIT 11

1 PRE-READING

Look at the pictures. Listen to your teacher tell the story.

The Cheap Apartment

The apartment building on East 60th Street in New York City

It is 1986. Jean Herman lives in an apartment in New York City. Jean's apartment is small, but she likes it. The apartment is cheap; Jean pays only $200 a month.

Jean's apartment is in an old building. One day a big company buys the old building. The company wants to tear down the old building and build a skyscraper.

Some people from the company visit Jean. "We're going to tear down this building," the people tell Jean. "So, you have to move. Here is a check for $50,000. You can find a new apartment—a big, beautiful apartment."

"I don't want a new apartment," Jean says. "I like this apartment. I'm not going to move." Jean doesn't take the check.

The next day, the people come back with a check for $100,000. Jean doesn't take the check. "I'm not going to move," she says.

Every day the people come back with more money. Jean doesn't take their checks.

Finally, the people come with a check for $750,000. "*Please* take the money and move," the people say.

"I'm not going to move," Jean says. "Not for $750,000. Not for a million dollars. Not for ten million dollars. I like this apartment. It's my home."

All of Jean's neighbors in the old building move, but not Jean. She doesn't move, and the company doesn't tear down the building. The company builds a new skyscraper behind the old building.

Jean dies in 1992, but now there is an unusual skyscraper on East 60th Street in New York City. It is a big new skyscraper with an empty old building in front of it.

2 VOCABULARY

Match the words and the pictures. Write your answer on the line.

| build | check | move | old building | skyscraper | tear down |

1. _____build_____

2. _____

3. _____

4. _____

5. _____

6. _____

3 COMPREHENSION

UNDERSTANDING PRONOUNS

Who is it? What is it? Write the letter of your answer on the line.

__b__ 1. *She* lives on East 60th Street in New York.

____ 2. *It* is small and cheap.

____ 3. A big company buys *it*.

____ 4. The big company wants to build *it*.

____ 5. *They* visit Jean.

____ 6. People from the company want Jean to take *it*.

____ 7. *They* all move.

a. a skyscraper

b. Jean Herman

c. the old building

d. people from the company

e. Jean's neighbors

f. Jean's apartment

g. a check for $750,000

UNDERSTANDING THE MAIN IDEAS

Which sentence is correct? Circle *a* or *b*.

1. a. Jean's apartment is large and expensive.
   b. Jean's apartment is small and cheap.

2. a. A big company wants to tear down the old building and build a restaurant.
   b. A big company wants to tear down the old building and build a skyscraper.

3. a. Jean doesn't take the check for $750,000.
   b. Jean takes the check for $750,000.

4. a. Jean doesn't want to move because she likes her apartment.
   b. Jean doesn't want to move because she likes New York City.

5. a. The company builds a skyscraper behind the old building.
   b. The company builds a skyscraper one mile from the old building.

4 DISCUSSION / WRITING

This is the floor plan of Jean's apartment:

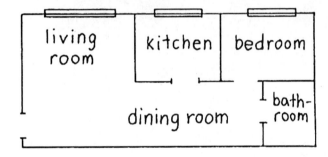

A On your own paper, draw the floor plan of your home. Under your drawing, write a few sentences about your home. For example:

I like our apartment, but it is too small. We have only one bathroom. Every morning we have the same problem: Who will go into the bathroom first?

B Show your floor plan to a classmate. Tell your classmate about your home.

UNIT 12

1 PRE-READING

Look at the pictures. Listen to your teacher tell the story.

Family for Rent

Mr. and Mrs. Sato are a little sad. It is a Friday afternoon, and they are thinking ahead to Sunday. Sunday afternoon is family time in Japan. But the Satos' daughter, son-in-law, and two grandchildren aren't going to visit them on Sunday. Their daughter and son-in-law both work full time, and they are too busy.

Mrs. Sato picks up the telephone and calls a company in Tokyo.

"Hello," a woman answers.

"Hello," Mrs. Sato says. "I'd like to rent a family."

"What would you like?" the woman asks Mrs. Sato. "A son? A daughter? Some grandchildren?"

"I'd like to rent a daughter, a son-in-law, and a grandson," Mrs. Sato says.

On Sunday afternoon, two actors come to the Satos' house—a woman and a man. They bring their one-year-old son. The actors stay with the Satos for three hours. They all eat lunch, talk, and play with the baby. Then the actors go home. The Satos feel happy.

The Satos' daughter didn't have time to visit them, so they called Rent-a-Family. The company sends "families" to people's houses. The families are really actors. The actors visit for three hours. The cost is $1,000.

Most people rent families because they are lonely. Their children and grandchildren don't visit them. But some people rent families because they like the actors. One woman says, "I always argue with my son and daughter-in-law. But I never argue with my rented family. My family is OK. But my rented family is better!"

2 VOCABULARY

Write the correct word or words on the line.

ahead	argue	full time	I'd like	son-in-law

1. It is Friday, and the Satos are thinking about Sunday. They are

   thinking _____*ahead*_____ .

2. The Satos' daughter works eight hours a day. She works _____.

3. Mrs. Sato is polite, so she doesn't say, "I *want* to rent a daughter." She says,

   "_____ to rent a daughter."

4. The Satos' daughter is married. Her husband is the Satos' _____.

5. People who have different ideas sometimes _____.

3 COMPREHENSION

UNDERSTANDING QUESTION WORDS

Complete the sentences. Write your answer on the line.

1. Where do Mr. and Mrs. Sato live?

   They live in *Japan* _____.

2. How do they feel?

   They feel a little _____.

3. Why isn't their daughter going to visit them?

   She is too _____.

4. Who are the man and woman who come to the Satos' house?

   They are _____.

5. When do they come?

   They come on Sunday _____.

6. What do the Satos do with them?

   They eat, talk, and play with the _____.

REVIEWING THE STORY

Write the correct word on the line.

Rent-a-Family is a _____*company*_____ in Tokyo, Japan. The company sends

1.

_____ to people's houses. The actors visit for three

2.

_____ . The _____ is $1,000.

3.   4.

Most people rent families because they are _____ . But some

5.

people rent families because they _____ the actors. They say, "My

6.

family is OK. But my rented family is _____!"

7.

4 DISCUSSION

Mr. and Mrs. Sato have a daughter. Her name is Yuko, and her husband's name is Kenji. Yuko and Kenji have two children, a boy named Takumi and a girl named Sakura. This is the Satos' family tree:

On your own paper, draw your family tree. Show it to a classmate. Tell your classmate about the people in your family.

5 WRITING

A **Read more about Mr. and Mrs. Sato.**

Mr. and Mrs. Sato are both 75 years old. They live in a house in Chiba, Japan. Every day they exercise, watch TV, use the Internet, and talk to their neighbors. Sometimes they feel a little sad because their daughter doesn't have time to visit them.

B **Imagine this: You are 75 years old. Where will you live? What will you do every day? How will you feel? Complete the sentences.**

1. I will live with _____ .

2. Every day I will _____

_____ .

3. I will feel _____ .

UNIT 13

1 PRE-READING

Look at the pictures. Listen to your teacher tell the story.

The Car in Row B

It is a busy Saturday morning for Max. He needs to mail two packages at the post office. He needs to return a book at the library. He needs to get cash at the bank. He needs to pick up some medicine at the drugstore. And he needs to buy a birthday present for his wife. He has a lot to do!

He gets in his car and drives downtown. He finds a big parking garage with six levels. He drives into the parking garage and finds a parking space. He parks his car in Row B. Then he takes the elevator down to the street.

Max mails two packages at the post office. He returns a book at the library. He gets cash at the bank. He picks up some medicine at the drugstore. Finally, he buys a birthday present for his wife.

Max walks back to the parking garage and takes the elevator up to Level 5. He walks to Row B. His car isn't there. He walks up and down the row, but he can't find his car. It is gone.

Max calls the police. "Somebody stole my car!" he says. The police look for Max's car for weeks, but they can't find it. Max buys a new car.

Twenty years later, the city decides to demolish the parking garage. Workers are walking through the garage. They are checking each level. The parking garage is empty. But on one level, the workers find an old car in Row B. They give the car's license number to the police. The police call Max. "Your car is in the parking garage!" the police tell him.

Why couldn't Max find his car on that busy Saturday morning? He was looking for it in Row B on Level 5. But he didn't park on Level 5. He parked in Row B on Level 4. And that is where his car stayed for twenty years.

2 VOCABULARY

Write the correct word on the line.

demolish	empty	gone	levels	space

1. Max finds a big parking garage. It has an elevator and six _____ *levels* _____.

2. Max finds a parking _____ in Row B.

3. Max can't find his car. It is _____.

4. The city wants to build a new parking garage. They are going to

   _____ the old one.

5. Workers want to be sure there are no cars or people in the parking garage. They

   are checking to be sure it is _____.

3 COMPREHENSION

UNDERSTANDING THE MAIN IDEAS

Circle the letter of your answer.

1. Why does Max park his car in the parking garage?
   - (a.) He has a lot of things to do downtown.
   - b. He works at a bank near the garage.

2. Why can't Max find his car?
   - a. He is looking for it on the wrong level.
   - b. Many cars are the same color.

3. How long is Max's car in the parking garage?
   - a. It is there for two weeks.
   - b. It is there for twenty years.

4. Where do workers find Max's car?
   - a. They find it on Level 4.
   - b. They find it on Level 5.

5. Who calls Max about his car?
   - a. The workers call him.
   - b. The police call him.

REMEMBERING DETAILS

What does Max need to do? Read his list. Write the missing words on the lines.

☐ mail two _____packages_____ at the post office

☐ _____ a book at the library

☐ get _____ at the bank

☐ pick up _____ at the drugstore

☐ buy a birthday _____

4 DISCUSSION

Max couldn't find his car.

A **What are things people sometimes can't find? For example, do people sometimes have trouble finding their shoes or keys? With your classmates, make a list. Your teacher will write your list on the board.**

B **How can people remember where their things are? Share your tips with the class.**

5 WRITING

Max has a lot to do: He needs to mail packages, return a library book, get cash, pick up medicine, and buy a present.

What are some things you need to do? Make a list on the lines below.

☐ _____

☐ _____

☐ _____

☐ _____

☐ _____

UNIT **14**

1 PRE-READING

Look at the pictures. Listen to your teacher tell the story.

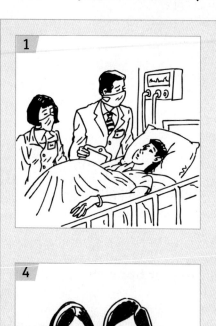

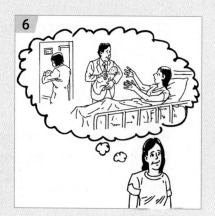

The Twins and the Truth

Petita Peña is scared. She is only 16 years old, and she is giving birth to her first baby. There are problems with the birth. Fortunately, she is in a hospital, and two doctors, a man and a woman, are helping her. They decide to do a cesarean.

When Petita wakes up from the surgery, she is happy. She has a beautiful baby girl. She names her daughter Andrea.

Andrea grows up in a town in Ecuador. When she is 14 years old, she and her parents go out to dinner in another city. At the restaurant, they see another girl. She is the same age as Andrea, with the same brown hair, the same brown eyes, and the same smile. The girls are identical.

The other girl is eating dinner with her parents. Who are her parents? They are Roberto Romo and Isabel Garcia—the married doctors who did the cesarean.

Later, Petita tells everyone, "The doctors lied to me! They told me, 'Congratulations! You have a beautiful baby girl!' But I had twin girls, not one girl! The doctors kept one of my babies!"

"That's not true!" the doctors say. "Yes, Petita Peña had twin girls. But she cried when we told her. 'I can't take care of two babies,' she said. So we kept one baby. We named her Marielisa. She is our daughter now."

Petita Peña and her husband tell Marielisa, "We want you to live with us." But Marielisa doesn't want to live with them. "I'll visit you and Andrea often," she tells them. "But I want to live with the doctors. They are giving me a good education, and they help me in every way. If you really love me, let me stay with them."

2 VOCABULARY

Which words have the same meaning as the words in *italics*? Write the letter of your answer on the line.

_e_ 1. Petita is *scared*.

_____ 2. *Fortunately*, she is at a hospital.

_____ 3. She gives birth to *twins*.

_____ 4. The two babies are *identical*.

_____ 5. She wakes up from the *surgery*.

_____ 6. The girls *grow up* in Ecuador.

a. luckily

b. two babies

c. exactly the same

d. operation in a hospital

e. afraid

f. live their early years

3 COMPREHENSION

REMEMBERING DETAILS

There are nine mistakes in the story below. Find the mistakes and cross them out. Choose the correct words and write them above the mistakes. The first one is done for you.

16	doctors	first	parents	scared
daughter	Fifteen	girl	restaurant	

scared

Petita Peña is ~~happy~~. She is only 18 years old, and she is giving birth to her

second baby. There are problems with the birth. Fortunately, she is in a hospital,

and two nurses are helping her. They decide to do a cesarean.

When Petita wakes up from the surgery, she has a beautiful baby boy. She

names her son Andrea.

Ten years later, Petita and her husband are at a park with Andrea. They see

another girl. She and Andrea are identical. The other girl is with her grandparents.

They are the doctors who did the cesarean.

LEARNING PAST TENSE FORMS

Match each verb with its past tense form. Write the letter of your answer on the line.

  c   1. do   a. had

_____ 2. tell   b. named

_____ 3. have   c. did

_____ 4. keep   d. lied

_____ 5. lie   e. told

_____ 6. cry   f. cried

_____ 7. name   g. kept

4 DISCUSSION

A Who do you think is telling the truth—Petita Peña or the doctors? Check (✓) your answer.

☐ I think Petita Peña is telling the truth.

☐ I think the doctors are telling the truth.

☐ I'm not sure.

B Explain your answer in a small group,

5 WRITING

A Play the game *Two Truths and a Lie* with your classmates. On the lines below, write three sentences about yourself—two that are true, and one that is a lie.

1. _____

2. _____

3. _____

B Read your sentences to the class. Can your classmates guess which sentence is a lie?

UNIT 15

1 PRE-READING

Look at the pictures. Listen to your teacher tell the story.

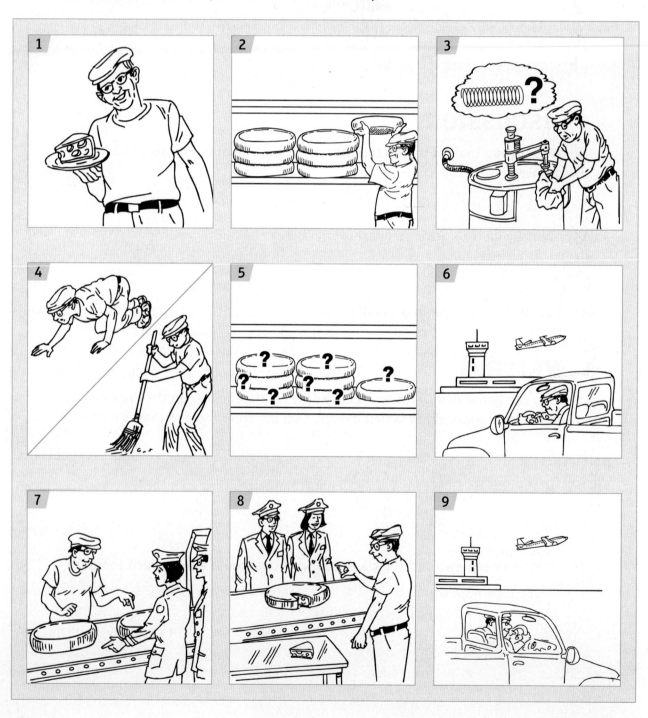

Quality Control

Fritz Ackerman is a cheese maker in Switzerland. Fritz is proud of his cheese. He thinks it is very good.

One day Fritz makes seven wheels of cheese. The wheels of cheese are big—each weighs 165 pounds (75 kilograms). They sell for $1,000 each.

Fritz wraps the cheese and puts it away. Then he begins to clean the machine that makes the cheese. He sees that a metal spring is missing from the machine. "It's probably on the floor," he thinks.

Fritz looks for the spring on the floor. He doesn't see it. He sweeps the floor. Then he sweeps it again. He doesn't find the spring. Where is it? It is probably in one of the wheels of cheese. But which one is it in?

Fritz thinks and thinks about his problem. Then he has an idea. He puts the cheese into his truck and drives to the airport. He takes the cheese to airport security. There is a big X-ray machine there. It looks for bombs in baggage.

It is a Tuesday afternoon, and the people who work in airport security are not busy. Fritz explains his problem to them. "Would you please run my cheese through the machine?" he asks.

"OK," they say. "We'll do it."

The X-ray machine finds the spring in one of the wheels of cheese. Fritz cuts into that wheel and takes out the spring.

"How much do I owe you?" Fritz asks the airport security workers.

"Nothing," they say. "We're happy to do it."

"Thank you!" Fritz says. He gives the cheese with the cut in it to the airport security workers. Then he puts the other six wheels of cheese into his truck and drives home. Fritz smiles all the way home. He is proud of his cheese. He *knows* it is very good.

2 VOCABULARY

Match the words and the pictures. Circle the letter of the answer.

1. Fritz is a cheese maker in *Switzerland*.

   (a.)    b.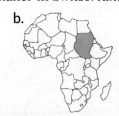

2. He makes *wheels* of cheese.

   a. 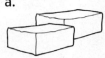   b.

3. Each *weighs* 165 pounds.

   a.    b.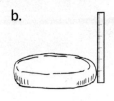

4. Where is the *spring*?

   a.    b.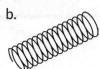

5. Fritz *sweeps* the floor.

   a.    b.

6. The machine looks for bombs in *baggage*.

   a.    b.

3 COMPREHENSION

MAKING CONNECTIONS

Find the best way to complete each sentence. Write the letter of your answer on the line.

1. Fritz looks for __c__   a. his truck.

2. He thinks about ____   b. the airport.

3. He puts the cheese into ____   c. the spring.

4. He drives to ____   d. one wheel of cheese.

5. Workers at security run the cheese through ____   e. his problem.

6. Fritz cuts into ____   f. an X-ray machine.

REMEMBERING DETAILS

There are ten mistakes in the story below. Find the mistakes and cross them out. Choose the correct words and write them above the mistakes. The first one is done for you.

1,000	big	cleaning	one	sweeps
airport	cheese	metal	seven	Switzerland

cheese

Fritz Ackerman is a ~~chocolate~~ maker in Sweden. One day he makes 70 wheels

of cheese. The wheels are big—each one weighs 165 pounds and sells for $100.

Fritz is repairing the machine that makes the cheese. He sees that a plastic

spring is missing. He washes the floor two times, but he doesn't find the spring.

Fritz takes the cheese to the factory. Workers there run the cheese through a small

X-ray machine. The machine finds the spring in two of the wheels of cheese.

4 DISCUSSION / WRITING

Fritz is proud of his cheese. What are you proud of?

A In the space below, draw a picture of someone or something you are proud of. Then complete the sentence below your picture.

I am proud of my _____

because _____.

B Share your picture and your writing in a small group.

UNIT 16

1 PRE-READING

Look at the pictures. Listen to your teacher tell the story.

Nothing's Changed

It is 1944. In a small town in Ukraine, Anton and Anna are asleep in their bed. They are a young married couple. Anton is 21, and Anna is only 15.

Suddenly soldiers come into the bedroom. They pull Anton out of bed. "Come with us!" the soldiers say. It is wartime, and the soldiers want Anton to be a soldier.

One year later, the war ends. After the war, Anton doesn't go back to Ukraine because he doesn't like the government there. He goes to New York City. Anton doesn't write Anna from New York. Anton thinks, "Maybe the police will ask Anna, 'Where is your husband?' If she doesn't know, it is better for her."

Anton is right: The police come to Anna's house and ask her, "Where is your husband?"

"I don't know," Anna says.

"Tell us!" the police say.

"I don't know," Anna says.

For the next nine years, the police come to Anna's house often. "Where is your husband?" they ask Anna. "Tell us!" Finally, Anna marries someone else. The police stop coming to her house.

Anton writes Anna. "I am in New York," he writes. "Come." But it is too late. Anna has a new husband now. She becomes a mother, and later she becomes a grandmother.

In 1994, Anna's husband dies. She writes Anton a letter. "I am free now," she writes. "Do you still have something in your heart for me?"

"Yes, I do," Anton writes back. "I never married again. I loved only you. Come to New York."

Anna arrives at the airport in New York City. She looks for Anton. There he is! After 50 years, there he is! But Anton walks past

Anna and Anton

Anna. Anton remembers his young wife. But he sees only a woman with gray hair.

"Anton!" Anna says.

"Anna?" Anton asks.

"Yes," Anna answers.

Anton opens his arms wide. "My Anna!" he says.

After 50 years apart, Anton and Anna are together again. "We're very happy," Anton says. "Same like before. Nothing's changed."

2 VOCABULARY

Write the correct word or words on the line.

apart	asleep	changed	couple	free	someone else

1. Anton is Anna's husband, and Anna is Anton's wife. They are a married _____couple_____ .

2. Men come into Anton's bedroom late at night. Anton is _____ in his bed.

3. Anton writes Anna from New York. "Come," he writes. But Anna cannot come because she has a new husband. She is married to _____ .

4. In 1994, Anna's husband dies, and she can marry Anton. "I am _____ now," she writes.

5. Anton says, "Nothing is different. Nothing's _____ ."

6. From 1944 to 1994, Anton and Anna were not together. They were _____ .

3 COMPREHENSION

UNDERSTANDING THE MAIN IDEAS

Complete the sentences. Write your answer on the line.

1. Where do Anna and Anton live in 1944?

   They live in _Ukraine_____ .

2. Why do men take Anton from his house?

   They want him to be a _____ .

3. Where does Anton go after the war?

   He goes to _____ .

4. Why doesn't Anton return to Ukraine?

   He doesn't like the _____ .

5. What does Anna answer when the police ask her, "Where is your husband?"

   She answers, "_____ ."

6. Why does Anton walk past Anna when she is at the airport in New York?

   He remembers his young wife, and he sees only _____ .

UNDERSTANDING TIME RELATIONSHIPS

When does it happen? Put a check (✓) under 1944, 1945, or 1994.

	1944	1945	1994
1. Anton goes to New York.	☐	✓	☐
2. Soldiers take Anton from his bed.	☐	☐	☐
3. Anna's husband dies.	☐	☐	☐
4. The war ends.	☐	☐	☐
5. Anna goes to New York.	☐	☐	☐
6. It is wartime in Ukraine.	☐	☐	☐

4 DISCUSSION / WRITING

Anton goes away. Where is he? Anna doesn't know. She waits nine years. Finally, she marries someone else.

A Imagine this: Your husband (or wife) goes away. Where is he (or she)? You don't know. How long will you wait before you marry someone else? Check (✓) your answer.

☐ 1 year

☐ 2 years

☐ 5 years

☐ 10 years

☐ forever

B Complete the sentence.

I will wait _____ because _____

_____

_____

C Read your sentence aloud in a small group.

UNIT 17

1 PRE-READING

Look at the pictures. Listen to your teacher tell the story.

An Accidental Success

It is a hot August evening in 1853. George Crum is working at a restaurant in Saratoga, New York. He is the chef, and he is very tired. He looks at the clock on the wall. It is eight o'clock. "One more hour," George thinks. "Then I can go home."

The doors of the kitchen open, and a waiter walks in. He is carrying a plate of potatoes. "The customer doesn't like the fried potatoes," the waiter says. "He wants them thin and crisp."

George makes some thin, crisp potatoes, and he gives them to the waiter. A few minutes later, the waiter returns with the potatoes. "The customer doesn't like them," the waiter says. "He wants them thinner and crisper."

George is angry. He cuts two potatoes into paper-thin slices. He fries them in hot oil until they are brown. He puts salt on them. Then he puts *more* salt on them. "Here!" he says to the waiter. "Extra-thin, extra-crisp potatoes. Extra salty, too!"

After the waiter leaves, George thinks about the potatoes and smiles. They are too salty and too brown. They are also too thin; it is impossible to eat them with a fork.

A few minutes later, the waiter walks back into the kitchen with an empty plate. "He loves them, and he wants more!" the waiter says. "Everybody at his table loves them, too."

George begins to make thin, crisp, salty potatoes at the restaurant every evening. They are a big success—a lot of customers come to the restaurant. Five years later, George opens his own restaurant and makes the potatoes there. Chefs at other restaurants begin to make the potatoes, too. Later the potatoes are made in factories, and they become popular all over the United States.

Today George's potatoes are popular all over the world. But we don't call them "George's potatoes." We call them "potato chips."

2 VOCABULARY

In the story, there are people, things, and food you can find in a restaurant.

Find the people, things, and food in the story. Write the words you find on the lines.

PEOPLE	THINGS	FOOD
customer		

3 COMPREHENSION

UNDERSTANDING THE MAIN IDEAS

Circle the letter of the best answer.

1. The customer doesn't like the potatoes because they are
   a. too salty.
   b. not thin and crisp.
   c. cold.

2. George makes potatoes for the customer
   a. two times.
   b. three times.
   c. four times.

3. Finally, George makes potatoes that are impossible to
   a. fry in oil.
   b. carry on a plate.
   c. eat with a fork.

4. The potatoes are extra thin, extra crisp, and extra
   a. salty.
   b. spicy.
   c. large.

5. The customer
   a. loves them and wants more.
   b. wants the waiter to try them.
   c. sends them back to the kitchen.

6. Today people eat "George's potatoes"
   a. only in Saratoga, New York.
   b. only in the United States.
   c. all over the world.

FINDING INFORMATION

Read each question. Find the answer in the paragraph below and circle it. Write the number of the question above the answer.

1. How is the weather?
2. What month is it?
3. What year is it?
4. What is George's last name?
5. Where is George working?

6. In what state is the restaurant?
7. What is George's work at the restaurant?
8. How does George feel?
9. What time is it?
10. Where does George want to go?

                                            1

    It is a (hot) August evening in 1853. George Crum is working at a restaurant in Saratoga, New York. He is the chef, and he is very tired. He looks at the clock on the wall. It is eight o'clock. "One more hour," George thinks. "Then I can go home."

4 DISCUSSION

Potato chips are popular all over the world. (In some English-speaking countries, people call them "crisps.")

Discuss the answers to these questions with your classmates.

1. What food from your country is popular in other countries?

2. Does it look and taste the same in other countries? If not, how is it different?

3. Do people in other countries say the name of the food correctly? If not, say it correctly for the class.

5 WRITING

A With the class, write a conversation between the waiter in the story and the customer. Your teacher will write the conversation on the board. Copy it on your own paper.

B Read the conversation aloud with a partner. If you would like to, read it with your partner in front of the class.

UNIT 18

1 PRE-READING

Look at the pictures. Listen to your teacher tell the story.

Something from Home

Amira loves her home, and she loves her country. But she has to leave. There is a war in her country, and it is dangerous to stay.

Amira and her husband decide to leave with their two children. They can take only two small suitcases. Amira looks around her home. What will she take with her? She packs clothes and jewelry. She packs family photos and important papers.

In her kitchen Amira has mixing bowls and spoons. She has baking pans and cookie sheets. Amira loves to bake. She wants to take everything. But she can't.

Amira has a wooden cookie mold. She uses it to make cookies. It is from her mother. Amira puts it in her suitcase.

Amira and her family leave their home. They are refugees now. First, they go to a refugee camp. They live there for four years. Then they go to the United States.

People in the United States help Amira. They give her many things. Amira gives them coffee and cookies. She makes the cookies with her mother's cookie mold.

"The cookies are delicious!" people say. "Maybe you can sell them." Amira makes 500 cookies. She sells them at a local music festival. In three hours, she sells all the cookies. "Maybe I can sell cookies at other festivals," she thinks. "Maybe I can sell them to coffee shops and grocery stores, too. And maybe I can sell them online." She needs a bigger kitchen.

Amira rents a commercial kitchen. Everything in the kitchen is new. But she has something old, too. She has her mother's wooden cookie mold.

Every Tuesday there is a farmer's market in Amira's new city. People sell many things at the market—vegetables, fruit, and flowers, for example. On Tuesdays Amira sells her cookies at the market. The market is open from 11 a.m. to 3 p.m. Amira sells all her cookies by 1 p.m.

Will Amira's cookie business be a success? We don't know the end of this story. But we know the beginning. It begins with a wooden cookie mold. It begins with something from home.

2 VOCABULARY

Match the words and the pictures. Write your answer on the line.

cookie sheets	jewelry	mixing bowl	refugee camp	spoons	suitcase

1. _____*spoons*_____ 2. _____ 3. _____

4. _____ 5. _____ 6. _____

3 COMPREHENSION

REVIEWING THE STORY

Write the correct word on the line.

Amira has to leave her country because there is a _____*war*_____. She
                                                          1.

and her family can take only two small _____. Amira puts a
                                                2.

wooden cookie mold from her _____ in her suitcase.
                                        3.

Amira's new home is in the United States. People there help her and her family.

They give them things for their home, and Amira gives them _____
                                                                        4.

and cookies.

People tell Amira her cookies are _____. Amira wants to sell
                                            5.

her cookies, so she rents a _____ kitchen.
                                    6.

Will Amira's cookie business be a _____? We don't know the
7.

end of the story. But we know the _____. It begins with a wooden
8.

_____ mold.
9.

LOOKING FOR INFORMATION

Find the words in the story. Copy them in the correct column.

Things in Amira's suitcase	Things in Amira's kitchen	Where Amira wants to sell her cookies
clothes		

4 DISCUSSION / WRITING

When Amira leaves her country, she packs her mother's wooden cookie mold.

A **Imagine this: You are going to live in another country. With your classmates, make a list of special things from home to take with you—pottery, a flag, or perfume, for example. Your teacher will write your list on the board.**

B **Draw one special thing to take with you. Draw a picture of it inside the suitcase to the right.**

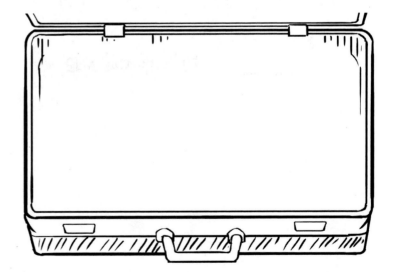

C **Complete the sentence.**

I will pack _____ because _____

_____ .

D **Share your drawing and your sentence in a small group.**

UNIT 19

1 PRE-READING

Look at the pictures. Listen to your teacher tell the story.

The Exchange

Every evening at six o'clock, Julio Diaz takes the New York subway home from work. After he gets off the subway, he goes to a small, inexpensive restaurant for dinner. Then he goes home.

One evening Julio gets off the subway at his station. He is walking to the stairs when a teenager stops him. The teenager has a knife in his hand.

"Give me your wallet," the teenager says. Julio gives him his wallet, and the teenager walks away.

"Wait a minute!" Julio says. "Come back!" The teenager turns around. He is surprised.

"Take my jacket, too," Julio says. "It's warm."

"Why are you doing this?" the teenager asks.

"Well, I think you really need money," Julio says. "Maybe you need a warm jacket, too. And maybe you're hungry. I'm going to a small restaurant near here for dinner. Do you want to come with me?"

"OK," the teenager says.

Julio and the teenager go to the restaurant. After they sit down, the manager and the waiters come to their table. "Hi, Julio!" they say. Then the dishwashers come to their table. "Hi, Julio!" the dishwashers say. "Hi!" Julio says. He knows everybody's name, and he talks to everybody.

Julio and the teenager eat dinner and talk. "Do you own this restaurant?" the teenager asks.

Julio laughs. "No," he answers. "But I come here almost every day."

"You're nice to everybody," the teenager says.

"Yes," Julio answers. "If you're nice to people, they're nice to you."

After dinner, the check comes. Julio looks at the check and then looks at the teenager. "I can't pay for dinner," he tells him. "You have my wallet."

The teenager gives the wallet to Julio, and Julio pays the check. Then Julio puts $20 on the table. "That's for you," Julio says.

"But I want something in exchange. I want your knife."

The teenager takes the money and puts it in his pocket. Then he puts his knife on the table and walks out the door.

2 VOCABULARY

Complete the sentences with the words below.

almost	exchange	inexpensive	near	owns	teenager

1. Julio pays only $8.95 for his dinner. The restaurant is _____ *inexpensive* _____.

2. Julio goes to the restaurant every day after work, but he doesn't go there on Saturday or Sunday. He goes there _____ almost _____ every day.

3. The young man who stops Julio is 14 or 15 years old. He is a _____ teenager _____.

4. The restaurant is not far from the subway station. "It's _____ here," Julio tells the teenager.

5. The teenager thinks, "Maybe this is Julio's restaurant. Maybe he _____ it."

6. Julio gives the teenager $20, and the teenager gives him something in _____.

3 COMPREHENSION

UNDERSTANDING THE MAIN IDEAS

Which sentence is correct? Circle *a* or *b*.

1. Every evening at six o'clock, Julio Diaz
   a. takes a taxi home from work.
   b. takes the subway home from work.

2. One evening a teenager stops Julio and says,
   a. "Give me your watch."
   b. "Give me your wallet."

3. Julio offers the teenager
   a. his jacket.
   b. his cell phone.

4. Julio and the teenager go to
   a. a store together.
   b. a restaurant together.

5. Julio knows all the people there because
   a. he goes there almost every day.
   b. he is the manager.

6. Julio gives the teenager $20, and the teenager gives him
   a. his knife.
   b. his address.

UNDERSTANDING CONTRACTIONS

The words below are in the story. What do they mean? Write your answer on the line.

1. it's _____it is_____

2. you're _____

3. I'm _____

4. they're _____

5. that's _____

4 DISCUSSION / WRITING

Julio gives the teenager his wallet and offers him his jacket. Then he asks him, "Do you want to eat dinner with me?"

A **Is it a good idea to talk to a robber? What do you think? Check (✓) your answer. Then complete the sentence you checked.**

☐ Yes, it is a good idea because _____

_____

_____.

☐ No, it is not a good idea because _____

_____

_____.

B **Share your answer in a small group.**

UNIT 20

1 PRE-READING

Look at the pictures. Listen to your teacher tell the story.

The Gift

Nisha Sharma

Today is Nisha Sharma's wedding day. She is going to marry a young man named Tapan. She is wearing a red wedding dress, and her hands and feet are painted with henna.[1] Musicians are playing, and flower girls are welcoming the 1,500 guests. It will be a big wedding!

Ten minutes before the wedding, Tapan's mother tells Nisha's father, "Pay my family $25,000, or Tapan won't marry your daughter."

"$25,000?" Nisha's father says. "I have gifts for your family—two refrigerators, two TVs, and two air conditioners. I have two of everything because you want gifts for Tapan's brother, too. And I have a car for Nisha and Tapan. But now you want more?"

"Yes," Tapan's mother says. "We also want $25,000 in cash, or we're calling off the wedding."

In India, there is a wedding custom: The bride's family gives gifts to the groom's family. So Nisha's father has gifts for Tapan's family. But now, just minutes before the wedding, Tapan's mother wants one more gift—money.

Nisha's family is angry. "You want many expensive gifts," they tell Tapan's family. "And now you want money, too?" The families begin to shout at one another and push one another.

Nisha watches the two families and thinks, "Does Tapan's family want a daughter-in-law? Or do they want expensive gifts? Does Tapan want me? Or does he want my father's money?"

"I'm calling off the wedding!" Nisha says.

"Please go home," Nisha's father tells Tapan's family. "Tell your guests to go home, too."

Six months later, Nisha marries someone else. It is a small wedding at her house. Nisha's parents don't give the groom's family refrigerators, TVs, air conditioners, or a new car. They give them only one gift— their daughter, Nisha.

---

1 Henna is a red-orange dye. It is made from the leaves of a plant. Please see the photo on page 81.

2 VOCABULARY

Match the definition and the word. Write the letter of your answer on the line.

_b_ 1. someone you invite to your home   **a.** bride

_____ 2. a present; something you give to someone   **b.** guest

_____ 3. a woman who is getting married   **c.** push

_____ 4. a man who is getting married   **d.** groom

_____ 5. to speak in a loud voice   **e.** gift

_____ 6. the opposite of pull   **f.** shout

3 COMPREHENSION

REVIEWING THE STORY

Write the correct word on the line.

Today is Nisha Sharma's _____wedding_____ day. She is going to
1.

_____ a young man named Tapan.
2.

Nisha's father has many _____ for Tapan's family. He has
3.

_____ of everything because Tapan's family wants gifts for
4.

Tapan's _____, too. But Tapan's family wants more. They want
5.

$25,000 in _____. If Nisha's father doesn't pay them, they will
6.

_____ off the wedding.
7.

Nisha's family is _____. The two families begin to
8.

_____ at one another and push one another. Nisha calls
9.

_____ the wedding. Six months _____, she
10.   11.

marries someone _____.
12.

REMEMBERING DETAILS

What gifts does Nisha's father have for Tapan and his family? Check (✓) four things. The first one is done for you.

☑ 1. two refrigerators

☐ 2. two microwave ovens

☐ 3. two TVs

☐ 4. two air conditioners

☐ 5. two computers

☐ 6. a house

☐ 7. a car

4 DISCUSSION / WRITING

A **Read the sentences about wedding customs in India.**

1. The bride wears a red, pink, or gold dress.

2. The bride's hands and feet are painted with henna.

3. The bride's family gives gifts to the groom's family.

B **Write about three wedding customs in your country. Write your sentences on the lines below.**

1. _____

   _____

2. _____

   _____

3. _____

   _____

C **Share your writing in a small group.**

ANSWER KEY

VOCABULARY   page 4

  2. CPR
  3. gone
  4. credit card
  5. free
  6. meals

UNDERSTANDING THE MAIN IDEAS   page 4

  2. b   3. a   4. a   5. b

UNDERSTANDING SEQUENCE   page 5

  2. 1, 2
  3. 2, 1
  4. 1, 2
  5. 1, 2

VOCABULARY   page 8

  2. sister-in-law
  3. shoveling
  4. gone
  5. dump
  6. empty

UNDERSTANDING THE MAIN IDEAS   page 8

  2. a   3. b   4. b   5. a

REMEMBERING DETAILS   page 9

  old onions
  old shoes
  empty cans
  old potatoes
  old clothes
  the coat

UNIT 3

VOCABULARY page 12

2. can't
3. a lot
4. young
5. husband
6. marry

REMEMBERING DETAILS page 12

2. b   3. b   4. a   5. b   6. a   7. b   8. b

WHO SAYS IT? page 13

2. a   3. a   4. c   5. d   6. b

UNIT 4

VOCABULARY page 16

2. hit
3. roll over
4. seat belt
5. hold on
6. wires

MAKING CONNECTIONS page 16

2. e   3. f   4. a   5. d   6. b

UNDERSTANDING SEQUENCE page 17

2. 1, 2
3. 2, 1
4. 2, 1

UNIT 5

VOCABULARY page 20

2. groceries
3. forest
4. feed
5. sign
6. through

REMEMBERING DETAILS   page 20

2. They take bread from babies.
4. They go into apartments through open windows.
6. They take fruit from kitchen tables.
8. They open cans of beer.

REVIEWING THE STORY   page 21

2. problem
3. near
4. must
5. city

UNIT 6

VOCABULARY   page 24

2. Russia — country
3. Joseph Stalin — leader
4. pants, shirt, dress — clothes
5. rabbit — animal
6. berries — fruit
7. sister, father, cousin — family
8. hammer, saw, nails — tools

REMEMBERING DETAILS   page 24

2. ~~friend~~ / leader
3. ~~woman~~ / man
4. ~~OK~~ / dangerous
5. ~~happy~~ / afraid
6. ~~photos~~ / pans
7. ~~big~~ / small
8. ~~days~~ / years

UNDERSTANDING SEQUENCE   page 25

2. 2, 1
3. 2, 1
4. 2, 1

UNIT 7

VOCABULARY   page 28

2. spreads
3. quickly
4. take off
5. anyway
6. put down

UNDERSTANDING THE MAIN IDEAS   page 28

2. a   **3.** a   **4.** b

FINDING MORE INFORMATION   page 29

2. e   **3.** c   **4.** a   **5.** b

UNIT 8

VOCABULARY   page 32

2. f   **3.** c   **4.** a   **5.** e   **6.** d

UNDERSTANDING SEQUENCE   page 32

2. 2, 1   **3.** 1, 2   **4.** 2, 1

WHO SAYS IT?   page 33

2. d   **3.** c   **4.** e   **5.** a

UNIT 9

VOCABULARY   page 36

2. pet
3. anymore
4. it doesn't matter
5. manager
6. quietly

UNDERSTANDING THE MAIN IDEAS   pages 36–37

2. b   **3.** b   **4.** a   **5.** b

UNDERSTANDING DIALOGUE   page 37

2. a   **3.** d   **4.** b

UNIT 10

VOCABULARY   page 40

2. airplane landing
3. climb
4. wheel
5. airplane taking off
6. field

MAKING CONNECTIONS   page 40

2. h   **3.** e   **4.** g   **5.** a   **6.** d   **7.** f   **8.** b

REMEMBERING DETAILS page 41

2. ~~windows~~ / wheels
3. ~~north~~ / east
4. ~~forest~~ / ocean
5. ~~time~~ / temperature
6. ~~jacket~~ / shirt

UNIT 11

VOCABULARY page 44

2. skyscraper
3. check
4. old building
5. move
6. tear down

UNDERSTANDING PRONOUNS page 44

2. f   3. c   4. a   5. d   6. g   7. e

UNDERSTANDING THE MAIN IDEAS page 45

2. b   3. a   4. a   5. a

UNIT 12

VOCABULARY page 48

2. full time
3. I'd like
4. son-in-law
5. argue

UNDERSTANDING QUESTION WORDS page 48

2. sad
3. busy
4. actors
5. afternoon
6. baby

REVIEWING THE STORY page 49

2. actors
3. hours
4. cost
5. lonely
6. like
7. better

UNIT 13

VOCABULARY   page 52

2. space
3. gone
4. demolish
5. empty

UNDERSTANDING THE MAIN IDEAS   page 52

2. a   3. b   4. a   5. b

REMEMBERING DETAILS   page 53

return
cash
medicine
present

UNIT 14

VOCABULARY   page 56

2. a   3. b   4. c   5. d   6. f

REMEMBERING DETAILS   page 56

2. 18 / 16
3. second / first
4. nurses / doctors
5. boy / girl
6. son / daughter
7. Ten / Fifteen
8. park / restaurant
9. grandparents / parents

LEARNING PAST TENSE FORMS   page 57

2. e   3. a   4. g   5. d   6. f   7. b

UNIT 15

VOCABULARY   page 60

2. b   3. a   4. b   5. b   6. a

MAKING CONNECTIONS   page 60

2. e   3. a   4. b   5. f   6. d

REMEMBERING DETAILS page 61

~~Sweden~~ / Switzerland

~~70~~ / seven

~~$100~~ / $1,000

~~repairing~~ / cleaning

~~plastic~~ / metal

~~washes~~ / sweeps

~~factory~~ / airport

~~small~~ / big

~~two~~ / one

UNIT 16

VOCABULARY page 64

2. asleep
3. someone else
4. free
5. changed
6. apart

UNDERSTANDING THE MAIN IDEAS page 64

2. soldier
3. New York City
4. government
5. I don't know
6. an old woman with gray hair

UNDERSTANDING TIME RELATIONSHIPS page 65

2. 1944
3. 1994
4. 1945
5. 1994
6. 1944

UNIT 17

VOCABULARY page 68

PEOPLE	THINGS	FOOD
customer	plate	potatoes
chef	fork	oil
waiter	table	salt

UNDERSTANDING THE MAIN IDEAS page 68

2. b　　3. c　　4. a　　5. a　　6. c

FINDING INFORMATION   page 69

2. August
3. 1853
4. Crum
5. at a restaurant
6. New York
7. chef
8. tired
9. eight o'clock
10. home

UNIT 18

VOCABULARY   page 72

2. cookie sheets
3. jewelry
4. mixing bowl
5. refugee camp
6. suitcase

REVIEWING THE STORY   pages 72–73

2. suitcases
3. mother
4. coffee
5. delicious
6. commercial
7. success
8. beginning
9. cookie

LOOKING FOR INFORMATION   page 73

Things in Amira's suitcase	Things in Amira's kitchen	Where Amira wants to sell her cookies
clothes	mixing bowls	festivals
jewelry	spoons	coffee shops
family photos	baking pans	grocery stores
important papers	cookie sheets	online
the wooden cookie mold		

UNIT **19**

VOCABULARY page 76

2. almost
3. teenager
4. near
5. owns
6. exchange

UNDERSTANDING THE MAIN IDEAS pages 76–77

2. b   3. a   4. b   5. a   6. a

UNDERSTANDING CONTRACTIONS page 77

2. you are
3. I am
4. they are
5. that is

UNIT **20**

VOCABULARY page 80

2. e   3. a   4. d   5. f   6. c

REVIEWING THE STORY page 80

2. marry
3. gifts (or presents)
4. two
5. brother
6. cash
7. call
8. angry
9. shout
10. off
11. later
12. else

REMEMBERING DETAILS page 81

3. two TVs
4. two air conditioners
7. a car

CREDITS

PHOTO CREDITS

Page 3: Courtesy of the Honolulu Star Advertiser; **7:** RoJo Images/Shutterstock; **11:** Antonio Guillem/123RF; **15:** Fred Farmer/AP Images; **19:** Jevgenia Issakova/123RF; **23:** Daseaford/Shutterstock; **27:** Shinja jang/Shutterstock; **31:** Africa Studio/Shutterstock; **35:** Malcolm Harris/Pearson Education Ltd; **39:** Bettmann/Getty Images; **43:** Alex Brandon/AP Images; **47:** Hideki Yoshihara/Aflo Co., Ltd./Alamy Stock Photo; **51:** Singhanart/Shutterstock; **55:** JGI/Tom Grill/Blend Image/Getty Images; **59:** Andrey Rudakov/Bloomberg/Getty Images; **63:** Photo of Anton and Anna Nakonecznyj Copyright © 2018. Hartford Courant. Used with Permission; **67:** 06photo/Shutterstock; **69:** Givaga/Shutterstock; **71:** Tanya Stolyarevskaya/Shutterstock; **75:** Rorem/Shutterstock; **79:** Sebastian John/AP Images; **81:** Sergey Potiyko/123RF.